For more information, address:
thecheekychimpsbooks@gmail.com

FIRST EDITION

Illustrations by Lauren Scott

ISBN 978-1-8380490-0-3 (Paperback)

Published by The Cheeky Chimps Books
www.thecheekychimpsbooks.com

THE CHEEKY CHIMPS GO TO THE OPTICIANS

by Sachin Shah

Illustrated by Lauren Scott

The Cheeky Chimps Books

Felix and Felicity were watching their favourite film when their mum noticed that they were sitting very close to the TV.

She asked them to sit further away from the TV.

'Now it looks blurry!' Felix complained.
Mum said, 'It's time for you to visit the opticians.'

Mum made an appointment for them for the next day.

Felicity was excited but Felix was feeling a bit nervous.

'You don't need to worry about going to the optometrist,' Mum said to Felix.

'That's the name for someone who tests people's eyes to make sure they are healthy and they can see well. It's going to be fine, I promise.'

The next day, they all sat in the waiting area.

It was very busy.

'Felix and Felicity!' the friendly optometrist called out.

'Nice to meet you both. First I'll need to check your eyes here, and then I'll take you through for your eye tests.'

'Now, sit still without moving your head and have a look into this machine.

Tell me what you can see.'

They could see a picture of a colourful hot-air balloon.

'Look at that picture for five seconds: 1 . . . 2 . . . 3 . . . 4 . . . 5.
Well done! Now it's time for your eye test.'

Mum explained to the optometrist why they had come.

Felix and Felicity took it in turns to sit in the big chair.

The optometrist used an object called an "occluder" to see how well their eyes worked together.

He waved the occluder and covered each eye: first, while they focused on the opposite wall, and then when they focused on something near.

'Now I'm going to look into the back of your eyes using this special equipment.

It won't hurt, but the light will be quite bright.'

Whilst the optometrist looked into their eyes,
Felix and Felicity were asked to look in different directions.

UP . . . DOWN . . . LEFT . . . RIGHT.
It was fun and they both giggled.

Next, the optometrist gave them each something fun to look at to help test their eyes.

'Wow! Look at the wings!' said Felicity.
'I think I can see the number twelve!' said Felix.

They then had to look into a mirror opposite them, which showed a chart on the wall.

On this chart, the optometrist chose to show them either letters or pictures.

These were big at the top and small at the bottom.

'Just try your best to read as many as you can,' the optometrist said.

Felicity was able to read everything clearly.

Felix couldn't read the smaller letters,
so the optometrist decided to do another test.

Very gently, the optometrist squeezed some drops into Felix's eyes.

It felt strange at first, and then made everything blurry for a while.

Felix was very brave.
The optometrist checked his vision once again.

This time, he told Felix he needed glasses to help him to see better.

Felix was much more relaxed now, and eager to try on some glasses.

'You've done very well,' the optometrist said, smiling at them.
'You can choose a sticker each.'

In the shop, Felix tried on lots of pairs of glasses to see which ones fitted him the best.

Some were too big, some were too small . . .
but some fit him just right.

Felix chose a blue pair of glasses.
He looked really cool in them and they felt very comfortable.

He was asked to come back to collect them once his lenses had been put into the frame.

The following week they returned to the opticians. Felix was really excited to try on his new glasses. They came in a bright case and with a soft cloth so he could clean them and look after them.

Later that day, Felix and Felicity sat down to watch their favourite film.

'Wait!' said Felix. 'I need to get my glasses!'
This time, Felix didn't need to sit too close to the TV,
and he could see perfectly!

He was very glad that he had gone to the opticians,
and he loved his new glasses.

JOIN US ON OUR NEXT ADVENTURE SOON...

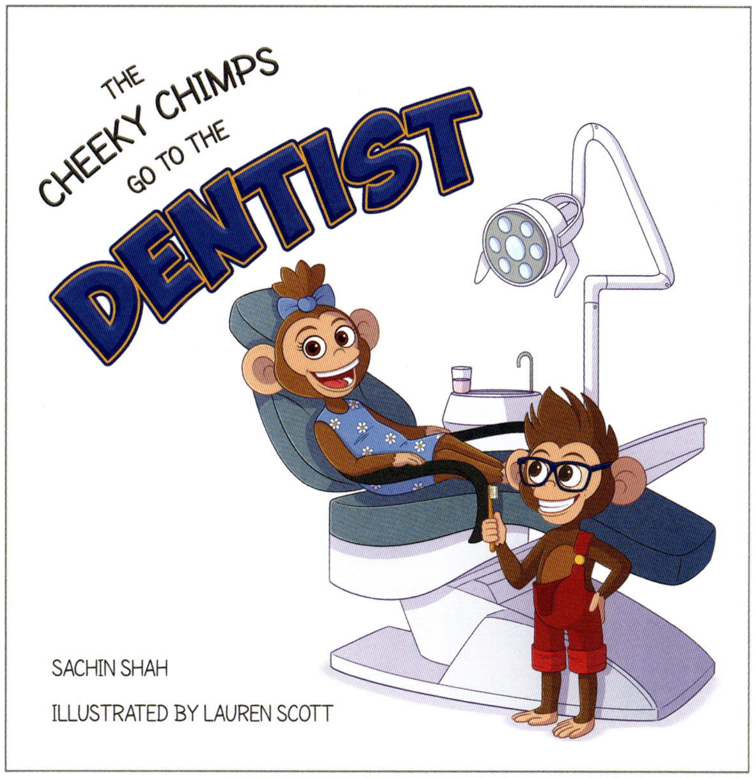

Visit **www.thecheekychimpsbooks.com**

for more information, fun activities or if you would like to get in touch!